Making Room for Excellence

Leadership for Public Servants

By L.S. Martin

Contents

Chapter 1: The Definition of Excellence

Chapter 2: Understanding Leadership

Chapter 3: Creating a Culture of Excellence

Chapter 4: Identifying and Nurturing Talent

Chapter 5: Empowering Your Team

Chapter 6: Leading with Purpose

Chapter 7: Overcoming Obstacles to Excellence

Chapter 8: Sustaining Excellence

Chapter 9: Conclusion

Introduction

"Leadership is not about titles, positions, or flowcharts. It is about one life influencing another" -- John C. Maxwell

Explanation of the book's purpose and how it will benefit readers

In writing this book, it was never my goal to put together a University-Level research document for peer review or publishing in a journal. This began as an attempt to put my thoughts, notes and experiences as a manager, leadership student and public servant for 2.5 decades together in a coherent form.

My hope is that this serves as an introduction to leadership for public servants from multiple fields. The goal was to make this general enough to be applicable for both the managing social worker and the supervising maintenance staff. My hope is that this book becomes a topic of conversation amongst co-workers which leads to better processes and practice.

I believe this to be a crucial time for this material to be made public. Primarily because there appears to be a leadership crisis in the ranks of public service. Public trust has eroded due to public institutions failing to evolve and service delivery being negatively impacted. This has created an existential crisis in many areas previously thought to be untouchable. Particularly in Law

Enforcement and Social Service arenas, recent social justice upheavals and de-funding movements have created a moment where these institutions must greatly change the way business is conducted; and any delay in the process will not be tolerated.

What is being demanded by the public is a culturally competent service delivery model which is effective, efficient, responsive, and flexible. None of this can or ever will be accomplished by public service managers performing business as usual. What is needed in this moment is effective leadership which can right the ship in terms of service delivery; and restore public trust in systems that appear outdated, broken, wasteful and harmful to the public good.

Hopefully this serves as part of the solution.

Overview of the book's contents

This book will examine the process of making room for excellence. We will discuss the foundations of leadership and how it differs from management. Next, we will discuss the benefits of creating a culture of excellence. This includes how to select talent and build a positive work culture, while avoiding common pitfalls. Lastly, we will discuss how to make these changes "sticky", so that they aren't easily lost over time.

Our goal is to delve into the key principles and strategies needed to foster excellence within public service organizations. This book offers valuable insights and practical guidance for leaders, managers, and individuals working in the public sector.

Firstly, we need to emphasize the importance of setting a clear vision and mission for public service organizations. By defining a compelling purpose, leaders can inspire and align their teams towards achieving excellence. The subsequent chapters explore the significance of creating a culture of continuous improvement and innovation, where individuals are encouraged to challenge the status quo and embrace change.

There is a critical role for leadership in promoting excellence. There are qualities and behaviors that effective leaders exhibit, such as visionary thinking, empathy, and the ability to empower and motivate others. Simply put, leadership can positively influence organizational performance.

Additionally, we must discuss the topic of talent management and highlight the need for attracting, developing, and retaining top talent in public service. Strategies for identifying and recruiting individuals with the right skills and mindset are explored, along with the significance of ongoing training and professional development to nurture talent within the organization.

Another key theme addressed in the book is the importance of embracing diversity, equity, and inclusion.

The author argues that organizations that value diversity and provide equal opportunities for all employees are more likely to achieve excellence. Strategies for fostering an inclusive and supportive work environment are discussed, along with the benefits of diverse perspectives and experiences in problem-solving and decision-making.

Public service organizations exist in a rapidly changing world. This book begins the discussion into strategies for managing complexity, navigating uncertainty, and adapting to evolving demands. The author emphasizes the need for agility, resilience, and the ability to learn from failures and setbacks.

Key to all these strategies is effective communication, both internally and externally. This cannot be understated. The use of transparent and open communication channels provides opportunities for collaborative decision-making and building trust among stakeholders.

Lastly, the book explores the role of technology and digital transformation in public service. It discusses the potential of emerging technologies to improve service delivery, streamline processes, and enhance citizen engagement. If we want to drive excellence public service organizations must embrace innovation and leverage technology.

Chapter 1:
The Definition of Excellence

"Perfection is not attainable, but if we chase perfection, we can catch excellence" – *Vince Lombardi*

Excellence in a leadership context

What is excellence?

If you were to look in the dictionary, or ask an online search engine for the definition of "excellence", you would get some version of the following:

"Excellence is a state of exceptional quality, performance, or achievement". And though the aforementioned is true and valid, it is not the whole story. The preceding definition is essentially outcome-based. Meaning that excellence could only be judged by the end product. I am looking to move beyond this narrow definition into something a bit more inclusive and intentional.

I want to add into my working definition some amount of consideration for the willingness to undertake journey itself, regardless of whether the destination is ever reached. By this, I'm referring to the pursuit of, and dedication to the highest standards of performance in one's endeavors. The willingness to go above and beyond what is expected; striving for perfection (though we may never achieve it) and continually improving oneself and one's work. And into this mix, I want to add a healthy dose of resilience and optimism.

During my time in public service, I have rarely, if ever, had sufficient resources required to have excellent outcomes. Most of the time we find ourselves in some version of attempting to do the most, while having the least. Therefore, If I only recognize the outcomes and neglect the process, I believe I'm doing a great disservice to the thousands of individuals who are furiously chasing after greatness while essentially being barefooted. New York Rapper 50 Cent might have said it best in the title of his movie, "Get Rich or Die Trying". Some of us in public service will, despite our best efforts, be in the "Die Trying" cohort.

To seek after excellence involves a combination of skills, knowledge, attitudes, and behaviors that enable individuals and organizations to consistently seek after, and hopefully achieve, outstanding results. Excellence is associated with dedication, commitment, discipline, creativity, innovation, and a passion. We need a strong work ethic, a growth mindset, a willingness to learn, and a focus on continuous improvement.

Concerning leadership, we want managers, captains, coaches, administrators, and supervisors to consistently demonstrate outstanding performance in moving their team towards achieving their goals. To do this you will need to inspire, motivate, and guide employees in being exceptional. There must be a commitment to continuous learning and growth, as well as a focus on developing and empowering team members to reach their full potential.

Ultimately, we want to create a culture of excellence within the organization. And always remember that just as an army is a collection of individual soldiers all doing their job… the work organization is essentially a collection of individual employees. They can thrive in an environment where high performance is expected and celebrated. Where team members are encouraged to collaborate, innovate, and take ownership of their work.

We know excellence in leadership when we see it. This is because it not only achieves exceptional results, but it does so while building and supporting a positive work environment that enables individuals and teams to thrive.

Chapter 2:
Understanding Leadership

"Leadership is not about being in charge. It is about taking care of those in your charge." -- Simon Sinek

"If your actions inspire others to dream more, learn more, do more, and become more, you are a leader" -- John Quincy Adams

Public Service Leadership

Being a leader in public service means taking on the responsibility of serving the community and promoting the common good. This is a special brand of leadership which seeks service over self. Private sector leaders may be focused on profits or creating shareholder value as the "bottom line". In contrast, the public servant's focus should be driven by a sense of purpose and a commitment to making a positive impact on society. They must be collaborative, ethical, inclusive, innovative, and results-oriented to achieve their mission and promote the common good.

When assuming a leadership role in public service, the responsibility to serve the community and work towards the betterment of society becomes a fundamental aspect of the position. Public service leaders are entrusted with the task of representing the interests of the people they serve and striving to make a positive impact on their lives. They play a vital role in shaping policies, implementing programs, and overseeing initiatives that address societal challenges and promote the common good.

The reader of this book is someone who aspires to leadership. Which means that they are likely to be focused on their own self development and growth. But remember that a leader is only as good as their team. In that regard, we should divert for a moment to focus on the profiles of individuals who would choose a public service career.

Choosing a career in public service is a decision that can be fulfilling and meaningful for individuals who have a genuine desire to make a positive impact on society. Each individual employee has their own "why" in terms of their reasoning for taking a job in the public sector. And of course, there is no perfect employee, but the dream candidate for any public service job will have most of the following qualities:

Passion for Public Good. Individuals who have a strong passion for serving others and a deep commitment to the well-being of their community are often drawn to public service careers. They genuinely care about making a positive difference in people's lives and are motivated by the opportunity to contribute to the common good.

Desire for Impact. Similar to "passion" as listed above, those who aspire to create meaningful change on a larger scale often find public service careers appealing. They want to tackle societal issues, address systemic challenges, and work towards improving the lives of individuals and communities. People like these are driven by the desires to tackle huge issues like eradicating homelessness, ending child abuse, and creating criminal justice reform.

Strong Ethical Compass. Public service requires individuals with high ethical standards and integrity. Those who prioritize fairness, honesty, transparency, and accountability are well-suited for careers in public service. They are committed to making decisions that are in the best interest of the community and are willing to uphold ethical conduct.

Problem-Solving Orientation. Careers in the public sector often involve navigating complex challenges and finding innovative solutions. Individuals who possess strong problem-solving skills, critical thinking abilities, and a willingness to tackle difficult issues can excel in such roles. They are driven to identify and address the root causes of problems to bring about positive change.

Collaborative Mindset. Working with diverse stakeholders, including government agencies, community organizations, and citizens is often required of the civil servant. Those who are skilled at building relationships, fostering collaboration, and navigating different perspectives can thrive in this arena. They understand the value of partnerships and teamwork in achieving common goals.

Resilience and Adaptability. Public service can frequently be demanding, with changing priorities, tight deadlines, and complex situations. Individuals who are capable of switching tasks, being adaptable, and able to navigate challenges with grace are well-suited for such careers. They possess the ability to handle adversity, learn from setbacks, and continuously improve their skills.

Commitment to Lifelong Learning. Any field involving working with the public will be dynamic. This means that practitioners must stay informed about emerging trends, evolving policies, and new technologies. Those who have a passion for learning, seek professional development opportunities, and are open to acquiring new knowledge bases and skillsets are likely to thrive.

Looking at the multiple qualities detailed above; If your team of employees has most of these values, you have a goldmine of untapped talent and opportunity. There is potential for excellence, if we can just create the correct environment for it to thrive.

It is important to note that public service careers encompass a wide range of roles and sectors, including government, nonprofits, international organizations, and community-based organizations. Therefore, your specific career path and job duties could potentially be rigid and inflexible. It is possible that an army of talented individuals are locked into positions where they cannot shine.

We need leaders who can work out how to release that talent into the open. We need someone to make room for excellence.

What does mean to be a leader, anyway?

The Leader Vs Manager dichotomy is one which must be discussed here. We need both. But I rarely see a job posting for "Visionary Leader" or "Transformative Leader". Rather, we are continuously hiring for one form or another of manager, supervisor, auditor, or policy expert.

A manager is an individual who is responsible for overseeing and directing the work of a group of people towards achieving specific organizational goals and objectives. Managers typically have formal positions of authority within an organization, such as department heads, team leaders, or executives.

The primary responsibilities of a manager include planning, organizing, directing, and controlling resources such as people, finances, and materials. They are responsible for setting objectives, developing strategies, assigning tasks, and making decisions that impact the success of the organization. Managers are also responsible for managing budgets, allocating resources, and ensuring that deadlines are met.

Overall, we can sum up the role of manager as overseeing and coordinating the work process to make sure that stated goals and objectives are achieved. They keep the people and machines making whatever it is they are supposed to be making. The focus is on the production of outcomes.

Contrast to the role of leader, which has a much more of a people centered approach. To be a leader means to have the ability to influence and inspire others towards a common goal or vision. A leader is someone who takes charge, guides, and motivates individuals or teams towards achieving shared objectives.

Being a leader involves having a clear understanding of one's own strengths and weaknesses, as well as the strengths and weaknesses of those around them. It requires the ability to communicate effectively, to listen actively, and to provide guidance and support when needed.

Both leaders and managers have to make tough decisions, take calculated risks, and be accountable for the outcomes of those decisions. But a leader is one who sets the tone for the culture of the organization. They create a positive and inclusive work environment, and foster collaboration and teamwork.

Again, we need both. But if an organization is truly trying to move forward, they need leaders more than they need managers. For example, any Manger can enforce HR policy. But a real leader recognizes and values diversity, promotes respect, and empowers individuals to reach their full potential. This goes far beyond simply documenting people's policy failures.

Making things even more distinct is the fact that leadership is not necessarily limited to formal positions of authority or titles, but rather can be demonstrated through actions and behaviors that inspire and influence others. The Manager may have a title. But the real leader in each office or work unit may be the lowest ranking individual. The true leader is one who sets the tone, sets the example, and others take their cues from.

Once the manager undertakes the responsibility of pursuing leadership, there is potential for dynamic change!

Different leadership styles and their pros and cons

There are several different leadership styles that can be effective depending on the situation, the organization, and the individuals involved. We will examine 5 common leadership styles and give a short description of each, as well as their pros and cons.

Autocratic leadership is a leadership style in which the leader makes all decisions and directs all activities without seeking input or feedback from their team. The autocratic leader is often characterized as being highly directive, with a clear focus on achieving goals and objectives. They use their formal authority and power to make decisions and control the actions of their subordinates.

Autocratic leaders typically do not delegate authority or responsibility to their team, instead preferring to make decisions and give orders themselves. They expect strict compliance with their instructions and may be critical or even punitive towards those who do not follow them.

This leadership style can be effective in situations where quick decisions need to be made or when there is a need for strict control and accountability. For example, in military operations or emergency situations, autocratic leadership may be necessary to ensure swift and decisive action.

However, autocratic leadership can also have negative consequences. It can stifle creativity, innovation, and collaboration, as employees may feel discouraged or disengaged from their work. It can also lead to a lack of job satisfaction, as employees may feel powerless and unimportant.

Overall, autocratic leadership can be effective in certain situations, but it should be used judiciously and balanced with other leadership styles as needed to promote employee engagement and well-being.

Autocratic Leadership: Pros:

- Quick decision-making
- Clearly defined roles and responsibilities

- Efficient use of time and resources

Cons:
- Lack of employee engagement and participation
- Limited creativity and innovation
- Negative impact on employee morale and job satisfaction

Transformational leadership is a leadership style that focuses on inspiring and motivating followers to achieve high levels of performance and personal growth. Transformational leaders are typically seen as charismatic, energetic, and visionary, with a strong ability to communicate their vision and ideas to others.

Transformational leaders work to empower their followers by providing a sense of purpose, meaning, and direction. They encourage creativity and innovation, and they actively seek out opportunities to develop and grow their team members' skills and capabilities. They also build strong relationships with their followers, fostering a sense of trust, respect, and loyalty.

Transformational leadership can be highly effective in organizations that value creativity, innovation, and collaboration. It can promote high levels of job satisfaction, engagement, and productivity, as well as enhance the quality of relationships between leaders and their followers.

However, transformational leadership can also have some potential downsides. Transformational leaders may be too focused on their vision and may not be willing to listen to others' ideas or feedback. Additionally, the high level of energy and engagement required from transformational leaders can lead to burnout and exhaustion, both for the leader and their followers.

Overall, transformational leadership can be a powerful tool for creating positive change and achieving high levels of performance, but it should be used judiciously and balanced with other leadership styles to ensure that the needs of both the organization and its employees are met.

Transformational Leadership: Pros:

- Inspiration and motivation of employees
- Encouragement of creativity and innovation
- Development of employee skills and potential

Cons:

- Potential for over-reliance on the leader
- Can be time-consuming and resource-intensive
- Requires a high level of trust between leader and employees

Situational leadership is a leadership style that involves adjusting one's leadership style based on the specific situation and the needs of the individuals or team being led. The Situational Leadership model, developed by Paul Hersey and Ken Blanchard, identifies four leadership styles that are appropriate for different levels of development of followers:

Directing: This leadership style is appropriate for followers who are new to a task or lack the necessary skills or experience. The leader provides clear instructions and closely supervises the follower's performance.

Coaching: This leadership style is appropriate for followers who are learning a new skill or task but still require a high level of direction and support. The leader provides guidance and feedback to help the follower improve their performance.

Supporting: This leadership style is appropriate for followers who have some experience and knowledge but may lack confidence or need reassurance. The leader provides support and encouragement to help the follower build their confidence and develop their skills.

Delegating: This leadership style is appropriate for followers who have the necessary skills and experience and can work independently. The leader delegates tasks and responsibilities to the follower and provides minimal supervision.

The Situational Leadership model emphasizes the importance of adapting one's leadership style to the specific needs of the situation and the followers being led. It recognizes that different followers may require different levels of direction, support, and delegation based on their level of experience and expertise.

Situational leadership can be an effective approach to leadership because it allows leaders to be flexible and responsive to the needs of their team. However, it can also be challenging because it requires leaders to be able to assess the development level of their followers and adjust their leadership style accordingly. It also requires a high level of communication and feedback to ensure that followers understand their roles and responsibilities and feel supported and empowered to achieve their goals.

Situational Leadership Pros:

- Flexibility and adaptability to different situations
- Customization of leadership style to individual or team needs
- Encourages employee development and growth

Cons:

- Requires a high level of communication and feedback
- Potential for confusion or uncertainty about expectations
- Can be time-consuming to implement effectively

Laissez-faire leadership is a hands-off approach to leadership where the leader delegates responsibility and decision-making authority to their subordinates. The term "laissez-faire" comes from the French phrase meaning "let do" or "let it be."

In laissez-faire leadership, the leader provides little guidance or direction to their team members, allowing them to work independently and make their own decisions. The leader may offer support and resources but generally does not interfere with the day-to-day activities of their team.

Laissez-faire leadership can be effective in certain situations, such as when team members are highly skilled and experienced, or when there is a need for creativity and innovation. It can also promote a sense of autonomy and empowerment among team members, which can lead to higher levels of job satisfaction and engagement.

However, laissez-faire leadership can also have its drawbacks. Without clear direction or guidance, team members may struggle to stay focused and motivated, leading to decreased productivity and quality of work. Additionally, in some cases, team members may not have the necessary knowledge or skills to make informed decisions, leading to mistakes or errors.

Overall, laissez-faire leadership can be effective in some situations, but it should be used carefully and only with highly skilled and motivated team members who can work independently. It should also be balanced with other leadership styles, such as coaching or directing, as needed to ensure that the team is meeting its goals and objectives.

Laissez-Faire Leadership: Pros:

- Encourages creativity and innovation
- Provides autonomy and empowerment to employees
- Can be effective in highly skilled or experienced teams

Cons:

- Lack of structure and guidance can lead to confusion or uncertainty
- Potential for lack of accountability and responsibility
- Can lead to a lack of productivity or progress

Servant leadership is a leadership philosophy that emphasizes the importance of serving others and putting their needs and interests first. In servant leadership, the leader sees themselves as a servant first and a leader second.

Servant leaders prioritize the needs of their team members, stakeholders, and communities and work to support their growth, development, and well-being. They focus on building relationships and creating a supportive environment that encourages collaboration, trust, and mutual respect.

Servant leadership is based on the belief that by serving others, leaders can create positive change and make a meaningful difference in the world. It is grounded in values such as empathy, humility, and compassion, and it places a high value on ethical behavior and social responsibility.

Some of the key characteristics of servant leadership include:

- Listening actively to others and seeking to understand their perspectives
- Empowering others to make decisions and take ownership of their work
- Creating a culture of trust and collaboration
- Focusing on the growth and development of team members
- Prioritizing the needs of others over their own needs or interests

Servant leadership can be effective in a wide range of contexts, from business and government to nonprofit and community organizations. It has been linked to higher levels of employee engagement, job satisfaction, and organizational performance.

However, servant leadership can also be challenging to implement, particularly in environments where there is a strong focus on hierarchy and power. It requires leaders to be willing to listen, be vulnerable, and put the needs of others first, even when it may not be in their own self-interest

Servant Leadership: Pros:

- Focus on employee needs and well-being
- Encouragement of teamwork and collaboration
- Promotes ethical and socially responsible behavior

Cons:

- Potential for overemphasis on employee needs to the detriment of organizational goals
- Can be time-consuming and resource-intensive
- Requires a high level of trust between leader and employees

Thoughts on Leadership Styles

The effectiveness of any leadership style depends on a variety of factors, including the organization, the situation, and the individuals involved. One of the most maligned styles in management literature is the autocratic style of leadership. It is typically held up as the example of how **not to** lead. Yet many of us who have played football, served in the military, or worked in emergency services can attest to the effectiveness of this style – in these specific arenas, under specific circumstances.

Contrastingly, it appears that Servant Leadership has been championed in leadership literature as a near universal cure-all for a myriad of organizational woes. I am a fan of this leadership stye and hope that all who work with me would identify this as my primary method. However, I believe that all leaders need to be flexible in their approach to truly be effective. When the building is on fire, there is no time to have a roundtable discussion of how we should escape and survive. The leader must reserve the right to be an autocrat and yell "Everybody get out, now!!".

A successful leader is one who can adapt their leadership style to meet the needs of their team, while still maintaining a focus on achieving organizational goals. You can and should have a favorite approach. But remember that rigidity is not a virtue when it comes to approach.

How to identify and develop your own leadership style

There are several ways to identify your leadership style. I advocate the use of 5 steps, the first four of which can be done in no particular order. If for some reason you cannot do all of these, I strongly advise the aspiring leader to not neglect step #5. I repeat, no matter what, complete step #5!! I believe this to be the most important of all.

Step #1: Self-reflection

Start by reflecting on your own behavior and actions as a leader. Consider your strengths, weaknesses, and tendencies in various leadership situations. Think about how you typically interact with others and how you approach decision-making and problem-solving. Are you a more take charge, directive leader? Do you typically require input from others before making a decision? Do your decisions mainly focus on doing the work, or revolve around the feelings of staff and employees?

Step #2: Feedback from others

Ask for feedback from your team members, colleagues, and others who have observed your leadership style. Ask them to describe your strengths and weaknesses as a leader and how they perceive your approach to leadership. One of the most effective evaluations is the 360 degree assessment. Seek to obtain input from subordinates, same level co-workers, and higher level managers regarding your leadership style.

Step #3: Leadership assessments

Take a leadership assessment, such as the Myers-Briggs Type Indicator or the DiSC assessment, to gain a better understanding of your leadership style and personality traits. There are multiple leadership tests available online for free or a nominal fee. Most provide some sort of leadership style assessment within just a few minutes.

Step #4: Observation of other leaders

Observe other leaders in your organization or industry and consider how they approach leadership. Identify the styles that resonate with you and consider how you could incorporate those elements into your own leadership style. In short, who do you admire for their leadership and wish you could be more like? What skills and traits do they have, which you would like to develop?

Step #5: Value Alignment

Once you have identified your leadership style, consider how it aligns with your personal values and the needs of your team and organization. Determine if there are areas where you could improve or develop new skills to be a more effective leader. Remember that leadership is a continuous learning process, and it is important to remain open to feedback and opportunities for growth and development.

More than once I have seen managers discover that their stated values and their actual leadership styles are not in sync. For example, if you claim to value stakeholder input, and use it to make good decisions, we have a problem if your assessment and co-worker feedback identifies you as primarily autocratic. In such cases, either the leadership behavior or the stated goals need to be modified.

Summary

Remember that leadership is a journey, and it is natural to experience some challenges along the way. By staying open to feedback, being flexible, and communicating openly, you can navigate these challenges and continue to grow as a leader.

Chapter 3:
Creating a Culture of Excellence

"Excellence is not an act but a habit. The things you do the most are the things you will do best." - Colin Powell

The importance of creating a culture of excellence within an organization

Creating a culture of excellence within an organization is essential for its success and long-term sustainability. It impacts employee motivation and engagement, innovation and creativity, reputation, and brand awareness, and determines whether the organization can continue to grow and evolve over time.

I once walked into a new seafood restaurant that opened near my home. It was located along a main street, near one of the busiest intersections in the city. Despite having good food and a fantastic location, the restaurant eventually shut down. Why? The service was terrible, the hours were unpredictable, and the prices were fairly high. In short, the culture and performance of this small business were lacking. And now, despite some of the best food around, the building sits vacant.

None of the readers of this book are likely to be running seafood shops. But the principal is the same. Creating a culture of excellence is crucial for organizational success. Public service carries the additional burden of its potential impact on society. In the paragraphs that follow, we will discuss several areas which can be positively impacted by undergoing the efforts to create a culture of excellence.

First and foremost, all governmental and public service organizations exist to serve the community and meet its needs. Creating a culture of excellence demonstrates a commitment to quality and accountability, which can enhance public trust and confidence in the organization.

Secondly, a culture of excellence can improve service delivery. This can provide an environment where team members are empowered to find innovative solutions, continuously improve processes, and collaborate across departments to achieve common goals.

Third, many public organizations are faced with unacceptably high employee turnover rates and morale issues. A culture of excellence can help address these by providing opportunities for growth and development, recognizing, and rewarding exceptional work, and fostering a sense of pride and purpose in the organization's mission.

Fourth, public service organizations are accountable for managing public resources effectively and efficiently. A culture of excellence can promote fiscal responsibility by encouraging team members to find cost-effective solutions, reduce waste and inefficiencies, and prioritize outcomes that deliver value to the community.

Lastly, governmental agencies have the power to make a significant impact on society. A culture of excellence can help ensure that this impact is both positive and long lasting. This culture can promote innovation, collaboration, and a focus on outcomes that meet the needs of the community.

In summary, creating a culture of excellence within a public service organization requires strong leadership, a commitment to transparency and accountability, and a focus on continuous learning and improvement. It also requires engaging team members, building trust with the community, and prioritizing outcomes that deliver value to the public. Failure to do so, jeopardizes the organizational missions and erodes the public trust.

Addressing this is particularly prudent in today's climate. Public Investigations of various entities designed to provide law enforcement, services to veterans, and child welfare have frequently exposed misconduct, lack of accountability and in some cases, corruption. Add to this a politically polarized environment, with a 24-hour news cycle, and the results can be devastating to an organization and the public.

Strategies for developing a culture of excellence

Now that we have established the need for a culture of excellence, we should discuss some strategies for implementation. There are some general strategies for developing a culture of excellence within any agency, whether public or private. Universally, organizations with a winning culture will have most, if not all the following 8 strategies functioning within the company:

1. Setting clear expectations and communicating values and standards for quality, integrity, and customer service.
2. Having a "Lead by Example" culture where managers model the behavior they want to see in their teams.
3. Fostering continuous learning through training, skill-building, and professional development.
4. Encouraging innovation and valuing creativity, experimentation, and appropriate risk-taking.
5. Recognizing and rewarding excellence through public recognition, bonuses, promotions, and other incentives.
6. Communicating and collaborating across teams, departments, and stakeholders.
7. Measuring and evaluating performance against established goals and benchmarks.
8. Promoting diversity and inclusion by fostering a culture where team members feel heard, valued, and supported.

Developing a culture of excellence in public service requires specific strategies that consider the unique challenges and opportunities in the public sector. In addition to the 8 strategies above, public service agencies will need to have strategies addressing several areas private entities might not be extremely concerned about.

A Customer Focused Culture

A customer-focused culture in public service is crucial for ensuring that services are designed and delivered with the needs and expectations of the public in mind. It involves adopting a mindset that places the customer at the center of all activities and decisions. Here we will discuss several key aspects of a customer-focused culture in public service; and how it can contribute to building a culture of excellence.

A customer-focused culture starts with a deep understanding of the needs, preferences, and challenges of the public. Public service organizations need to invest time and resources in gathering insights through surveys, focus groups, and direct engagement with the community. This understanding will enable them to develop services that are relevant and responsive to customer expectations.

Secondly, empathy and compassion is emphasized in all interactions with the public under a customer-focused culture. Public service professionals must be trained to listen attentively, show understanding, and provide support to individuals seeking assistance. This empathetic approach will help build trust and enhances the overall customer experience.

Transparency is the next cornerstone of a customer-focused culture. Public service organizations must ensure that information about services, processes, and decision-making is easily accessible to the public. They should provide clear and concise communication, avoiding jargon and technical language. Transparent communication helps customers understand what to expect and how to access services.

Next, a customer-focused culture values prompt and responsive service delivery. Any agency serving the public must establish processes to ensure timely responses to customer inquiries, requests, and feedback. They must set service standards and monitor performance to ensure that customers' needs are addressed in a timely manner.

Additionally, a customer-focused culture promotes a mindset of continuous improvement. Service organizations need to actively seek feedback from customers and use it to drive enhancements to their services. This encourages innovation and seeks to embrace new approaches to meet evolving customer needs. By continuously seeking to improve, organizations can deliver a higher quality service product that effectively serves the community.

Collaboration is also vital in a customer-focused culture. Agencies must recognize the value of working together with external stakeholders, such as community organizations, non-profits, and businesses. Through effective partnership, organizations can leverage resources, expertise, and networks to deliver comprehensive and integrated services that address complex societal challenges.

Further, a customer-focused culture recognizes the importance of personalizing services to meet individual needs. Public service organizations aim to provide tailored solutions that address specific customer circumstances. This may involve offering different service options, flexible delivery methods, or customized assistance to ensure that customers' unique requirements are met.

Lastly, a customer-focused culture involves setting performance metrics and holding public agencies accountable for their service delivery. Organizations must establish key performance indicators (KPIs) and regularly monitor their progress. Performance measurement allows organizations to track their effectiveness, identify areas for improvement, and demonstrate accountability to the public.

To conclude, a customer-focused culture in is built upon understanding customer needs, empathy, transparent communication, responsiveness, continuous improvement, collaboration, personalization, and accountability. An agency attempting to build a culture of excellence must attempt to embed these principles into their operations. In this way, public service organizations can create a culture that values and prioritizes the needs of the community, leading to enhanced service delivery and improved customer satisfaction.

Building Public Trust

Building trust in public service is essential for fostering strong relationships between public service organizations and the communities they serve. This is the second key to building a culture of excellence. Trust is the foundation of effective governance and public administration. Here we will examine some of the various aspects of building trust in public service:

As stated in the previous section, transparency is a cornerstone of building trust. All public agencies should strive to be open and transparent in their actions, decisions, and communication. This involves sharing information with the public, providing access to data and records, and explaining the reasoning behind policies and processes. Transparency builds confidence and credibility, showing the public that the organization has nothing to hide.

Next, all public agencies must demonstrate accountability for their actions. This includes taking responsibility for mistakes, admitting errors, and rectifying them promptly. By holding themselves accountable, organizations show their commitment to serving the public's best interests and maintaining high standards of ethics and integrity.

Clear and effective communication is always crucial for building trust. Public service organizations should communicate with the public in a timely and understandable manner. Communication should be two-way, encouraging dialogue and actively seeking feedback from the public.

Additionally, service agencies should strive to demonstrate competence and expertise in their areas of responsibility. By employing qualified professionals and continuously developing their skills, organizations can build trust by delivering high-quality services and making informed decisions. Competence inspires confidence and reassurance in the public.

Moreover, consistency and reliability in service delivery are crucial for building trust. Public agencies should strive to deliver services consistently and reliably, ensuring that the public can depend on them when needed. Consistency builds predictability and reliability, which are essential elements in establishing trust.

Building trust often involves collaborating with external stakeholders and forging partnerships. Public service organizations should actively engage with the community, other government agencies, and non-profit organizations to address complex issues collaboratively. By working together, organizations can leverage collective expertise, resources, and networks, thereby enhancing trust through shared responsibility and shared success.

A growing area of concern is privacy and data protection. In an era of data leaks and identity theft, protecting the privacy and personal information of the public is crucial for building trust. Public service organizations should establish robust privacy policies, adhere to data protection regulations, and ensure the secure handling of sensitive information. Respecting individuals' privacy rights and safeguarding their data demonstrates a commitment to their well-being and helps build trust.

Lastly, as stated in previous sections, a responsive and customer-centric approach is essential for building trust. Public service organizations should actively listen to the needs and concerns of the public, respond promptly to inquiries and requests, and continuously improve services based on feedback. By demonstrating a genuine commitment to customer satisfaction, organizations can instill trust and confidence in the public.

To wrap up, building trust in public service requires transparency, accountability, effective communication, competence, consistency, collaboration, privacy protection, and a customer-centric approach. This is the 2nd key area of ensuring an agency is fostering a culture of excellence. By embodying these principles, public service organizations can establish and maintain strong trust relationships with the public, leading to improved service delivery, increased public satisfaction, and enhanced public confidence in the institutions that serve them.

Empowering Employees

This topic is so important that it warranted having an entire chapter dedicated to it. We will examine it fully in chapter 5. However for the purposes of discussing how it relates to building out a culture of excellence, we will discuss it briefly here.

Empowering employees in public service is crucial for creating a motivated and high-performing workforce. Empowering employees begins with delegating authority and decision-making power to individuals at different levels within the organization. Carries through to providing opportunities for professional employee growth, and encouraging staff to think outside the box, finding innovative solutions to challenges.

An agency that empowers its employees is investing in building a culture of trust and accountability. This is a crucial part of building out a culture of excellence. For a full discussion of employee empowerment, see chapter 5.

Fostering Continuous Improvement

The next step in creating the culture of excellence is fostering continuous improvement. This is crucial for enhancing the efficiency, effectiveness, and responsiveness of any public agency. This will involve embracing a culture of learning, collecting and analyzing data, encouraging employee input, and multiple other key aspects. Below are some of the factors which must be focused on in order to move this forward:

As previously stated, fostering continuous improvement begins with creating a culture of learning within the organization. Leaders should promote a mindset that encourages employees to seek out opportunities for growth, share knowledge, and continuously develop their skills. This culture of learning fosters a proactive and innovative approach to problem-solving and encourages employees to identify areas for improvement.

Continuous improvement requires the collection and analysis of data to identify trends, patterns, and areas for enhancement. Public service organizations should establish mechanisms for collecting relevant data and employ analytical tools to derive insights. Data-driven decision-making helps identify gaps, inefficiencies, and opportunities for improvement.

There cannot be growth without encouraging employee input. Fostering continuous improvement involves actively seeking input and feedback from employees at all levels. Public service organizations should create platforms for employees to share their ideas, suggestions, and insights. By involving employees in the improvement process, organizations tap into their expertise and experience, promoting ownership and engagement.

Next, public service organizations should establish clear performance metrics and key performance indicators (KPIs) to track progress and measure success. These metrics provide a basis for assessing the effectiveness of processes, services, and initiatives. Regularly reviewing performance metrics helps identify areas for improvement and guides decision-making.

Further, the organization must examine process mapping and streamlining. Continuous improvement involves analyzing and streamlining processes to eliminate inefficiencies and bottlenecks. Public service organizations should engage in process mapping exercises to identify areas of improvement and implement strategies for enhancing efficiency and effectiveness. Streamlining processes leads to faster, more streamlined service delivery and reduces the risk of errors or delays.

Once again, collaboration is key!! Continuous improvement is enhanced through collaboration and knowledge sharing. Public service organizations should promote cross-functional collaboration, both internally and externally. Collaborating with other government agencies, community organizations, and stakeholders enables the sharing of best practices, lessons learned, and innovative solutions. Collaboration facilitates a collective approach to problem-solving and enables organizations to learn from others' experiences.

Next, continuous improvement requires a feedback loop that includes regular evaluation and assessment. Public service organizations should gather feedback from customers, employees, and other stakeholders to identify areas for improvement. Feedback should be used to inform decision-making and drive action. Regular evaluation ensures that improvement efforts are on track and helps organizations adapt to changing needs and priorities.

If an agency is truly committed to having a culture of excellence, they must be committed to continuous improvement. In the public service arena, this will require embracing a culture of learning, collecting and analyzing data, encouraging employee input, establishing performance metrics, process mapping and streamlining, encouraging innovation, promoting collaboration and knowledge sharing, and implementing feedback and evaluation mechanisms. By prioritizing continuous improvement, public service organizations can enhance their ability to meet the evolving needs of the public, deliver high-quality services, and drive positive change within their communities.

Embracing Technology

Embracing technology in public service has become essential for improving efficiency, enhancing service delivery, and keeping up with the changing needs of citizens. If an organization wishes to create a culture of excellence, they will need to remain nimble in integrating technological advances into their work. This section will discuss multiple key aspects needed to embrace technology in public service:

Embracing technology involves undertaking digital transformation initiatives within the organization. This includes digitizing processes, adopting digital tools and platforms, and integrating technology into service delivery. Digital transformations improve efficiency, reduce administrative burdens, and enable more seamless interactions with citizens.

Typically, the digital transformation will result in enhancements to an organization's service delivery mechanisms. Online portals, mobile applications, and self-service options provide citizens with convenient access to information and services. This is often associated with improved overall citizen experience and increased satisfaction levels. Embracing technology allows organizations to provide services efficiently and effectively, meeting citizens' expectations in a digital age.

One example of this can be found in the state of Colorado. The state has set a goal to be a "cloud first" state, according to Suma Nallapati, former CIO for the Governor's Office of Information Technology. The technology investments will likely pay dividends many years into the future, but it's already producing results now. By moving its Medicare/Medicaid eligibility program to the public cloud, the state sped up processing and approval times. Now, Coloradans spend less time waiting for their benefits.

Embracing technology also provides potential for data analytics and insights. Technology allows public service organizations to collect, analyze, and leverage data for decision-making and performance improvement. Data analytics tools can provide valuable insights into citizen needs, service usage patterns, and operational performance. This data-driven approach helps organizations identify areas for improvement, make informed decisions, and optimize resource allocation.

Next, technology improvements can enable automation of routine and repetitive tasks, freeing up resources for more value-added activities. Public service organizations can automate processes such as data entry, document management, and workflow management. Automation streamlines operations, reduces errors, and increases efficiency. This allows employees to focus on higher-level tasks and provide more personalized services to citizens.

Further, embracing technology can positively impact collaboration and communication efforts. Technology can facilitate collaboration and communication within and across public service organizations. Collaborative platforms, instant messaging tools, and video conferencing solutions enable teams to work together seamlessly, regardless of geographical locations. Embracing technology breaks down communication barriers, fosters knowledge sharing, and improves coordination among employees.

Of particular concern, are potential liabilities concerning cybersecurity and data privacy that come with new technological models. Embracing technology requires an organization to have a strong focus and commitment to protecting the data generated by such processes. Public service organizations must prioritize the protection of sensitive citizen information and ensure compliance with data protection regulations. Robust security measures, employee training, and regular assessments of IT systems are essential for maintaining trust and safeguarding citizen data.

Despite the aforementioned concerns, the benefits of increased public engagement appear to outweigh the risks of possible data leaks. Technology provides opportunities for increased public participation in the decision-making process. Public service organizations can leverage social media, online surveys, and interactive platforms to gather feedback, solicit ideas, and involve citizens in policy discussions. Embracing technology can empower citizens, promote transparency, and strengthen democratic processes.

Lastly, always remember that technology is constantly evolving, and public service organizations must embrace a culture of continuous innovation. By staying abreast of technological advancements, organizations can identify new tools, systems, and approaches that enhance service delivery and address emerging challenges. Embracing technology encourages a mindset of innovation and adaptability, driving continuous improvement within the public sector.

In conclusion, embracing technology in public service involves digital transformation, enhanced service delivery, data analytics, automation, collaboration, cybersecurity, public engagement, and continuous innovation. This builds the culture of excellence by allowing public service organizations to modernize their operations, improve citizen experiences, and respond effectively to the evolving needs of society. Embracing technology enables organizations to deliver more efficient and citizen-centric services, ultimately contributing to the overall well-being and progress of communities.

Diversity, Equity and Inclusion

A highly debated topic in the media over the past few years has been Diversity, equity, and inclusion (DEI). These are essential in public service to ensure fairness, representation, and equal opportunities for all individuals. If an agency wants to truly build a culture of excellence, DEI efforts must be considered and implemented. Here we will discuss some areas for potential organizational growth concerning DEI in public service.

To begin, all public service organizations should actively seek and embrace diversity in their workforce. This includes recruiting individuals from different backgrounds, experiences, and perspectives. Embracing diversity promotes creativity, innovation, and a broader range of ideas, enabling organizations to better understand and address the needs of diverse communities they serve.

Internally, this means agencies must establish inclusive policies that promote equal opportunities and eliminate barriers. This includes implementing fair hiring practices, providing equal access to training and development opportunities, and creating supportive work environments where all employees feel valued and respected. Inclusive policies ensure that diverse voices are heard and contribute to decision-making processes.

Externally, DEI efforts will require public employees to be trained in cultural competence to understand and appreciate the diverse cultures, beliefs, and values of the communities they serve. Cultural competence fosters effective communication, enhances service delivery, and builds trust between public service organizations and citizens. It helps prevent biases and promotes inclusivity in decision-making.

Additionally, making progress on DEI will require agencies to address bias and discrimination. This includes implementing policies and procedures to address complaints, promoting reporting mechanisms, and providing training on unconscious bias and discrimination. By addressing bias and discrimination, organizations create an environment where all individuals can thrive and contribute their full potential.

Another area that must be addressed is public service organizations demonstrating diverse representation in leadership positions. This includes ensuring equitable opportunities for career advancement and creating mentorship and sponsorship programs for underrepresented groups. Having diverse leadership promotes inclusivity, inspires others, and ensures that decision-making reflects the perspectives and needs of the entire community.

Furthermore, any agency involved in public service should be actively engaging with diverse communities to understand their needs and concerns. This involves conducting outreach programs, seeking feedback, and involving community members in decision-making processes. Engaging with diverse communities helps build trust, improves service delivery, and ensures that policies and programs address the specific needs of different populations.

For many organizations the above recommendations will require collection and analysis of available data concerning DEI indicators. This will identify service gaps and areas for improvement. This includes collecting demographic data on employees and applicants, analyzing representation at different levels, and monitoring outcomes to identify disparities. Data-driven approaches enable organizations to track progress, identify systemic barriers, and inform targeted interventions.

Nell Haslett-Brousse, director of diversity, equity & inclusion at Point B, a consultancy located in Boston, suggests that "The fundamental measures in detecting diversity gaps include workforce and leadership representation with comparative ratios by race, ethnicity, gender, gender identity, veteran status, presence of disability, LGBTQ+ identity, age group, management level and geographical location, if such is applicable". These are fairly simple and direct data queries.

To conclude, a culture of excellence in any service organization will need to include efforts at DEI. Diversity, equity, and inclusion are crucial in public service to foster fairness, representation, and equal opportunities for all individuals. By embracing diversity, creating inclusive policies, addressing bias and discrimination, promoting diverse representation in leadership, engaging with diverse communities, collecting and analyzing data, and prioritizing continuous learning, public service organizations can work towards creating more inclusive and equitable societies. Embracing DEI in public service not only enhances organizational effectiveness but also contributes to building a more just and equitable society for all.

Leading with Purpose

The next step to creating a culture of excellence is leading with purpose. Just like employee empowerment, this topic is important enough to have its own chapter. We will discuss leading with purpose in depth in chapter 6. Briefly though, we will discuss a few key tenets for the purposes of supporting a culture of excellence.

The first step of leading with purpose is having a clear and compelling mission that aligns with the organization's purpose. This must be communicated effectively to team members. Allow them to see the connection between their day-to-day work and the bigger Departmental mission. To support and reinforce this, decision makers must to embody and promote the values of public service, such as integrity, transparency, and accountability.

By leading with purpose, public service decision makers can inspire and guide their teams towards achieving meaningful goals, making a positive impact on society, and fostering a culture of excellence and service. For the full discussion on this topic, see chapter 6.

Building trust and fostering collaboration within teams

By now, you have read again and again that a culture of excellence requires teamwork, communication, collaboration and trust. But how do you build out trust and collaboration, particularly if the agency does not have this already at it's core?

In this section we will touch on this important topic. Particularly because building trust and fostering collaboration within teams in public service is crucial for achieving collective goals, enhancing effectiveness, and delivering quality public services. Here we will discuss some key aspects to consider when it comes to building trust and fostering collaboration within teams.

Everything begins with communication. We must encourage open and transparent communication among team members. This creates an environment where everyone feels comfortable sharing ideas, concerns, and feedback. Foster active listening and ensure that everyone's voice is heard and respected. Open communication builds trust and promotes collaboration by facilitating effective problem-solving and decision-making.

Secondly, the organization must set clear and shared goals that align with the overall mission of the agency. Staff have to know what they are doing, why, and how it connects to the mission. Involve team members in the goal-setting process to ensure their commitment and ownership. When individuals understand how their work contributes to the bigger picture, they are more likely to collaborate and work together towards achieving those goals.

Third, we must encourage team members to build positive relationships based on trust, respect, and mutual understanding. Promote a sense of camaraderie and encourage team-building activities. Strong relationships foster trust, enhance communication, and create a supportive environment where collaboration can thrive.

Fourth, leaders must recognize and appreciate the contributions of team members. Celebrate successes, acknowledge individual achievements, and express gratitude for the efforts of the entire team. When people feel valued and recognized, they are more motivated to collaborate and go the extra mile to achieve team goals.

Fifth, the organization must have a mechanism and culture of conflict resolution. Address disagreements within the team promptly and constructively. Encourage open dialogue, active listening, and empathy. Provide opportunities for mediation and foster a culture where conflicts are seen as opportunities for growth and learning. Resolving conflicts effectively strengthens trust and encourages collaboration.

Sixth, as stated in the previous section, the organization must promote diversity, and inclusion. If you want people to trust and collaborate, then the organization has to encourage diverse perspectives, ideas, and backgrounds. Create an inclusive environment where everyone feels valued and respected, regardless of their differences. Diversity and inclusion foster innovation, creativity, and collaboration by bringing different viewpoints and experiences to the table.

Next, we must seek to foster a culture of sharing information and resources among team members. Encourage knowledge-sharing, provide access to relevant data and resources, and promote cross-functional collaboration. Sharing information and resources eliminates silos, promotes collaboration, and enables teams to work more efficiently and effectively.

Lastly, the organization must seek to support professional growth and development of team members. When individuals are enhancing their expertise, they can contribute their knowledge and skills to the team. Continuous learning fosters collaboration by ensuring that team members are equipped with the necessary tools and knowledge to collaborate effectively.

To conclude this section, a culture of excellence will require the organization to build trust and foster collaboration within teams. This is crucial for achieving collective goals and delivering high-quality services. By promoting open communication, establishing shared goals, building relationships, recognizing contributions, addressing conflicts, promoting diversity and inclusion, sharing information and resources, and supporting continuous learning, public service organizations can create a collaborative and trusting environment where teams can thrive.

What we want is better problem-solving, improved decision-making, and ultimately, more effective, and impactful public service delivery.

Chapter 4: Identifying and Nurturing Talent

"Talent is the multiplier. The more energy and attention you invest in it, the greater the yield." - Marcus Buckingham

"The secret of my success is that we have gone to exceptional lengths to hire the best people in the world." - Steve Jobs

How to identify and recruit top talent

Identifying and recruiting top talent in public service is essential for building high-performing teams and ensuring effective delivery of public services. It all starts with the people. Leaders are advised to remember that teams, groups, and entire organizations are comprised of individual employees attempting to work towards a common goal. Picking the right people at the outset makes all the difference.

To begin, any organization hoping to recruit talent must start by clearly defining the role and responsibilities of the position you are looking to fill. Identify the skills, qualifications, and experience required for success in the role. This will help you establish the criteria to evaluate candidates and ensure that you attract the right talent.

Next, there must be a leveraging of professional networks, both internally and externally, to identify potential candidates. Leaders must reach out to colleagues, professional associations, and industry networks to seek recommendations or referrals. Networking is an effective way to connect with individuals who have the skills and expertise you are looking for.

It would be wise for organizations to make full use of online platforms and job portals to advertise their job openings. Platforms like LinkedIn, government career websites, and specialized job boards can help you reach a wider pool of candidates. Clearly articulate the job requirements and highlight the unique aspects of the public service environment to attract top talent.

Another way to find excellent candidates is to establish partnerships with universities and colleges that offer relevant programs. Engage with career centers, participate in job fairs, and consider internships or co-op programs to identify and recruit emerging talent. By building relationships with educational institutions, you can tap into a fresh talent pool and contribute to talent development.

In order to assess for the best candidates, public agencies should use a variety of assessment tools, such as interviews, tests, and case studies, to evaluate candidates' skills and competencies. Look beyond the traditional qualifications and focus on the candidate's potential to adapt, learn, and thrive in a public service environment. Consider behavioral and situational questions to gauge how candidates handle challenges and make ethical decisions.

In all recruitment efforts it is important to highlight the purpose and impact of public service in your recruitment process. Emphasize the opportunity to make a difference and contribute to the well-being of the community. Top talent is often attracted to organizations with a strong sense of purpose, so articulating the value of public service can help you appeal to candidates who are passionate about making a positive impact.

Additionally, high performing organizations should actively seek diverse candidates and create an inclusive recruitment process. Consider implementing blind recruitment practices that focus on skills and abilities rather than personal characteristics. Diversity brings different perspectives and experiences, which can enhance creativity, innovation, and problem-solving within the public service organization.

Once you have a pool of candidates, the agency must ensure that the recruitment process is efficient and streamlined. Communicate with candidates promptly, provide feedback, and keep them updated throughout the process. Lengthy and cumbersome selection processes can deter highly qualified candidates. A smooth and transparent process reflects positively on your organization and enhances the candidate experience.

In conclusion, identifying and recruiting top talent in public service requires a proactive and strategic approach. By defining the role, leveraging networks, utilizing online platforms, collaborating with educational institutions, assessing skills and competencies, promoting the public service mission, embracing diversity and inclusion, and streamlining the selection process, public service organizations can attract and secure top talent. Hiring individuals who possess the necessary skills, passion, and commitment to public service is crucial for building strong teams and delivering high-quality public services that meet the needs of the community.

Strategies for developing and nurturing talent within your team

Now that you have successfully recruited the best candidates available, how do we grow them into high performing employees? Developing and nurturing talent within your team in public service is crucial for maximizing performance, fostering growth, and ensuring long-term success. Here are eight strategies to consider when it comes to developing and nurturing talent within your team:

Identify Strengths and Development Areas: Take the time to assess the strengths and development areas of each team member. This can be done through performance evaluations, feedback sessions, and self-assessment tools. By understanding their individual strengths and areas for improvement, you can tailor development plans that capitalize on their strengths and address any skill gaps.

Provide Learning and Training Opportunities: Offer a variety of learning and training opportunities to support the professional development of your team members. This can include workshops, conferences, webinars, and online courses. Encourage team members to take advantage of these opportunities and provide the necessary resources and support to facilitate their learning.

Assign Challenging Projects: Provide team members with challenging and meaningful projects that allow them to stretch their abilities and gain new experiences. Assigning projects that align with their interests and developmental goals not only enhances their skills but also keeps them engaged and motivated. Ensure that they have the necessary support and resources to succeed in their assignments.

Mentoring and Coaching: Establish a mentoring and coaching program within your team. Pair more experienced team members with those who are looking to grow and develop. Mentors can provide guidance, advice, and support, while coaches can help individuals enhance specific skills and overcome challenges. This mentorship and coaching relationship helps nurture talent and fosters a culture of learning and growth.

Encourage Knowledge Sharing: Promote a culture of knowledge sharing within your team. Encourage team members to share their expertise, best practices, and lessons learned. This can be done through regular team meetings, brown bag sessions, or internal knowledge-sharing platforms. By creating an environment where knowledge is freely exchanged, you foster continuous learning and development among team members.

Recognize and Reward Progress: Acknowledge and recognize the progress and achievements of your team members. Celebrate milestones and accomplishments, both big and small. Recognizing their efforts and providing positive feedback boosts morale and motivates individuals to continue their development journey. Consider implementing a recognition program that rewards exceptional performance and growth.

Foster a Culture of Feedback: Create a culture where feedback is encouraged and valued. Provide constructive feedback regularly and in a timely manner. Encourage team members to seek feedback from their peers, supervisors, and subordinates. Feedback promotes self-awareness, helps individuals identify areas for improvement, and supports their professional growth.

Support Work-Life Balance: Recognize the importance of work-life balance in nurturing talent. Encourage team members to maintain a healthy balance between their professional and personal lives. Offer flexible work arrangements, promote well-being initiatives, and create an environment that prioritizes self-care. When individuals feel supported and have a healthy work-life balance, they are more likely to thrive and contribute their best.

To wrap up, developing and nurturing talent within your team in public service requires a proactive and holistic approach. By identifying strengths and development areas, providing learning opportunities, assigning challenging projects, fostering mentoring and coaching relationships, encouraging knowledge sharing, recognizing progress, fostering a culture of feedback, and supporting work-life balance, you can create an environment that promotes continuous learning, growth, and the realization of individual potential. Investing in the development of your team members not only enhances their skills and capabilities but also contributes to the overall success of your public service organization.

Providing feedback and support for individuals to achieve their full potential

Providing ongoing feedback and support is essential for helping individuals achieve their full potential. These strategies are applicable in many workplaces, but in public service the stakes may be higher. This is because public servants are often tasked with working with the poor, sick, elderly or other vulnerable populations. If we want to ensure these groups receive excellent care, from a highly skilled workforce, we must give our employees to the tools to be great.

To start, the organization must establish an environment where feedback is valued and encouraged. Employees and clients must have open lines of communication where they feel comfortable giving and receiving feedback. Leaders must regularly provide constructive feedback to help employees understand their strengths and areas for improvement. Encourage self-reflection and self-assessment to promote continuous learning.

Next, the organization must schedule regular performance conversations with each team member to discuss their progress, achievements, and areas for development. These must not be used only as "gotcha" meetings, where individuals are only given negative feedback. Leaders must use these conversations as an opportunity to set goals, align expectations, and provide guidance. By having ongoing discussions about performance, you can provide timely feedback and support for individual growth.

In order not to lose momentum from performance meetings, the discussion should be memorialized in Individual Development Plans (IDP). Leaders should work collaboratively with each team member to develop an IDP. Identify their career aspirations, skills they want to enhance, and areas they wish to explore. This plan should outline specific objectives, actions, and timelines for achieving their development goals. Regularly revisit and update the plan to ensure alignment with changing needs.

If the organization truly wishes for employees to reach their full potential, they must provide coaching and mentoring to support individuals' professional growth. Leaders should offer employees guidance, advice, and support to help them navigate challenges and overcome obstacles. Pair team members with experienced mentors who can provide valuable insights and help them develop new skills. Coaching and mentoring relationships foster personal and career development.

Another effective option is to encourage individuals to engage in continuous learning. Public service organizations should provide access to training programs, workshops, seminars, and online resources. Leaders should support employee participation in professional development opportunities that align with their goals and the needs of the organization. Promote a culture of learning and encourage individuals to share their learnings with the team.

As these learning opportunities culminate in milestones, the agency should celebrate employee achievements. Acknowledging individuals for their contributions, milestones, and successes publicly can boost morale, motivate individuals, and reinforce the value of their efforts. Take the time to highlight the impact of their work and demonstrate appreciation for their dedication.

Always remember that each employee is an individual; no two are alike. If we truly want to see them reach their full potential, we must ensure individuals have the necessary support and resources to excel in their roles. Provide access to tools, technology, and training that enable them to perform at their best. However, remember to attempt to tailor needed support to their unique needs and career aspirations. Recognize that everyone has different strengths and learning styles, and provide individualized support accordingly.

Lastly, the organization must encourage individual employees to build and leverage professional networks. Support their participation in industry events, conferences, and networking opportunities. These connections provide access to diverse perspectives, learning opportunities, and potential mentors. Encourage individuals to share their knowledge and expertise with others to enhance collaboration and collective growth.

To conclude this section, providing ongoing feedback and support is vital for helping individuals achieve their full potential in public service. By establishing a feedback culture, conducting regular performance conversations, creating individual development plans, offering coaching and mentoring, promoting continuous learning opportunities, celebrating achievements, providing tailored support and resources, and encouraging professional networks, you create an environment that fosters growth, engagement, and the realization of individual potential. When individuals feel supported and empowered, they are more likely to excel in their roles, contribute meaningfully to the organization, and make a positive impact in public service.

Chapter 5: Empowering Your Team

"The best executive is the one who has sense enough to pick good men to do what he wants done, and self-restraint enough to keep from meddling with them while they do it." - Theodore Roosevelt

The benefits of empowering your team

In theory, an individual who holds a supervisor, manager or formal leadership role was selected due to their ability to make sound decisions. So the question must be asked "Why would we let employees make their own choices?". The answer of course is that the manager cannot be omnipresent, and there are spillover benefits to employee empowerment. Some of these advantages are a more engaged workforce, a more nimble process and better overall outcomes.

We covered some of the benefits of empowering your team in the section on building a culture of excellence. In this section we will discuss more thoroughly, the significant positive outcomes this can have for public service organizations and their employees.

Here are several key advantages of empowering your team:

Increased Job Satisfaction: Empowering your team members gives them a sense of autonomy and ownership over their work. This leads to increased job satisfaction as they feel valued, trusted, and respected. When employees are satisfied with their roles, they are more likely to be motivated, engaged, and committed to achieving organizational goals.

Higher Productivity and Efficiency: Empowered team members are more motivated to excel in their work. They take initiative, make decisions, and find innovative ways to accomplish tasks. This leads to improved productivity and efficiency within the team and the organization as a whole. Empowered employees take responsibility for their outcomes and proactively seek opportunities for improvement.

Enhanced Creativity and Innovation: When team members are empowered, they feel comfortable sharing their ideas and opinions. This fosters a culture of creativity and innovation, where diverse perspectives are valued. Empowered employees are more likely to think outside the box, propose new solutions, and contribute to continuous improvement. This can lead to better problem-solving, decision-making, and service delivery.

Improved Employee Development: Empowering your team creates opportunities for personal and professional growth. By providing challenging assignments, delegating authority, and offering training and development resources, you enable your employees to expand their skills and capabilities. This not only benefits the individual but also enhances the talent pool within your organization.

Strengthened Collaboration and Teamwork: Empowered teams promote collaboration and teamwork. When employees are empowered to make decisions and contribute to the team's success, they are more likely to collaborate effectively with their colleagues. This leads to improved communication, coordination, and synergy among team members, resulting in higher-quality outputs and greater efficiency.

Enhanced Employee Engagement: Empowering your team fosters a sense of ownership and engagement among employees. They feel invested in their work and are more likely to go the extra mile to achieve results. Engaged employees are passionate about their roles, committed to the organization's mission, and willing to contribute their best efforts. This can lead to higher employee retention rates and reduced turnover.

Better Problem-Solving and Decision-Making: Empowering your team allows them to be involved in problem-solving and decision-making processes. By giving them the authority to make decisions within their areas of expertise, you tap into their knowledge and experience. This leads to more well-rounded perspectives, better-informed decisions, and effective solutions to challenges that arise in public service.

Improved Service Delivery: When team members are empowered, they are better positioned to meet the needs of the public they serve. Empowered employees have the flexibility and authority to respond promptly and effectively to customer inquiries, concerns, and requests. This leads to improved service delivery, increased customer satisfaction, and a positive reputation for your organization.

In conclusion, empowering your team in public service brings numerous benefits. It enhances job satisfaction, increases productivity and efficiency, fosters creativity and innovation, supports employee development, strengthens collaboration and teamwork, boosts employee engagement, improves problem-solving and decision-making, and enhances service delivery. By empowering your team members, you create a positive work environment where individuals can thrive, contribute their unique skills and perspectives, and drive the success of your public service organization.

Strategies for empowering team members to take ownership and responsibility

We want our employees to take ownership and responsibility for their work, advancing the organization mission, and serving the community. This is crucial for fostering a high-performing and engaged workforce in public service. In order to get there from our present state, here are several strategies to consider.

All empowerment starts by clearly defining each team member's role, responsibilities, and objectives. Leaders must ensure that everyone understands their areas of ownership and the expectations associated with their roles. When team members have a clear understanding of their responsibilities, they are more likely to take ownership and accountability for their tasks.

The second strategy to employ is empowering your team members by delegating authority and giving them the autonomy to make decisions within their areas of expertise. Provide guidelines and boundaries but allow them the freedom to explore different approaches and make choices. By delegating authority, you demonstrate trust in their abilities and encourage them to take ownership of their work.

The third strategy building employee empowerment is to offer professional development opportunities, such as training programs, workshops, and mentoring. Public service agencies must invest in their team members' growth and provide them with the resources and support they need to enhance their skills and capabilities. This empowers them to take ownership of their professional development and strengthens their ability to contribute to the team's success.

The fourth employee empowerment strategy is to encourage collaboration and shared decision-making. The organization must foster a collaborative work environment where team members can participate in decision-making processes. Encourage open communication, active listening, and the exchange of ideas. When team members feel that their input is valued and their perspectives are considered, they are more likely to take ownership of the team's outcomes and contribute their best efforts.

Further, there is no employee empowerment without the public service agency providing continuous feedback and recognition. Leaders must regularly respond to and recognize team members. Acknowledge their achievements, strengths, and areas of improvement. This feedback should be constructive, specific, and timely. Recognize their efforts publicly and privately, which not only boosts their morale but also reinforces their sense of ownership and responsibility.

An additional strategy to provide employee empowerment is to encourage a culture of continuous learning and innovation within your team. Emphasize the importance of embracing new ideas, seeking opportunities for improvement, and taking calculated risks. Encourage team members to think creatively, propose innovative solutions, and experiment with new approaches. By fostering a culture of learning and innovation, you empower your team members to take ownership of their growth and contribute to the team's success.

As a final strategy for employee empowerment, leaders must attempt to model the behavior they want to see from their team members. Public service agencies must expect that those in managerial roles demonstrate ownership, responsibility, and accountability in their actions. When employees see leaders taking ownership and being responsible, they will be more likely to do the same.

In conclusion, empowering team members to take ownership and responsibility is essential for creating a motivated and engaged workforce in public service. By implementing strategies such as clearly defining roles, delegating authority, providing growth opportunities, fostering collaboration, giving feedback, fostering a culture of learning, setting clear goals, and leading by example, you can empower your team members to excel in their roles, contribute their best efforts, and drive the success of your public service organization

Encouraging creativity and innovation within your team

Encouraging creativity and innovation within your public service team can lead to improved problem-solving, enhanced service delivery, and a more engaged and motivated workforce. In this section we will discuss several ways to foster creativity and innovation.

To begin, all agencies seeking to innovation must create a work environment that encourages open communication, respect for diverse ideas, and a sense of psychological safety. Leaders must ensure that team members feel comfortable expressing their thoughts and opinions without fear of judgment or criticism. We want employees and agency partners to be encouraged to think outside the box and take appropriate risks.

In order to accomplish the above, leaders must actively encourage their team members to generate and share their ideas. Regularly hold brainstorming sessions or idea-sharing forums where team members can contribute their thoughts and suggestions. Provide platforms or channels for team members to share ideas anonymously if they prefer. By actively seeking input and ideas from their team, leaders can create an environment that fosters creativity and innovation.

No amount of creativity can overcome a lack of basic resources. The organization must ensure that teams have access to the necessary people, tools, and technology to support their creative endeavors. This could include training programs, workshops, online resources, or access to innovative equipment. By providing the right tools and resources, you empower your team members to explore new ideas and approaches.

Noted Pastor and author Dan Carrol has said on several occasions, "Opportunity is spelled R.I.S.K.". In short, if we want people to connect with others and make bold innovations, we must embrace the possibility of failure. Leaders must therefore encourage their team members to take calculated risks and embrace experimentation.

The innovative public service organization will foster an environment where failures are seen as learning opportunities rather than mistakes. Leaders must support and celebrate innovative initiatives, even if they don't always yield the desired outcome. By supporting risk-taking, we create an environment that encourages creativity and innovation.

When employees do take the leap of faith and attempt something bold or creative, the agency should acknowledge and reward the effort. Leaders should publicly recognize individuals or teams who come up with creative solutions or implement innovative practices. This recognition not only celebrates their achievements but also reinforces the importance of creativity and innovation within the entire organization.

Finally, if we want creative things to happen, we must allow time to employees to think, dream and be imaginative. Leaders should allow your team members dedicated time for reflection and exploration. Encourage them to step back from their daily tasks to explore new ideas, trends, and developments within their field. This could involve attending conferences, engaging in professional development activities, or allocating time for research and learning. When an agency provides time for reflection and exploration, they create space for creativity and encourage innovative thinking.

To wrap up, encouraging creativity and innovation within your team in public service is essential for driving progress and improving outcomes. Agencies must foster a supportive environment, encourage idea generation, provide resources, embrace diversity, support risk-taking, empower decision-making, recognize innovation, and provide time for reflection and exploration.

This can all lead to a culture of creativity and innovation within your team and throughout the organization. This furthers our end goal of improved problem-solving, enhanced service delivery, and a motivated and engaged public service workforce.

Chapter 6:
Leading with Purpose

"Good leaders organize and align people around what the team needs to do. Great leaders motivate and inspire people with why they're doing it." -- Marillyn Hewson

The importance of having a clear sense of purpose as a leader

In 1519 Hernan Cortes left from the shores of Cuba headed to the Yucatan peninsula of Mexico. Cortes had 500 soldiers, 100 sailors and 16 horses loaded onto 11 ships funded by the Spanish crown. His mission was to engage and defeat the Aztec army which had not been defeated by an adversary in over 600 years. Vastly outnumbered and facing nearly insurmountable odds, Cortes instructed his army to burn the boats. There would be no retreat. Victory or death were the only two options.

I suspect that none of the individuals reading this are Spanish conquistadors seeking gold and jewels. Nonetheless, the principal remains that having a clear sense of purpose as a leader is crucial for inspiring and motivating your team, driving meaningful change, and achieving organizational goals. In this section we will discuss why having a clear sense of purpose is so important for agency culture and outcomes.

To begin, having a clear sense of purpose provides inspiration and motivation to both you and your team.

When you have a clear vision of the positive impact you want to create through your work, it becomes a driving force that energizes and motivates you and your team members to give their best efforts. You can think of this as the "why" regarding the "what" we are being asked to accomplish.

Secondly, having a sense of purpose serves as a compass that guides your decision-making process. It helps you make choices that align with your values, vision, and goals. When faced with complex or challenging decisions, having a clear sense of purpose helps you stay focused and make choices that support your larger objectives. When in doubt, we can always refer to the mission statement to guide us.

Thirdly, if leaders will commit to clearly communicating this purpose, the agency can rally teams around a common cause, inspiring them to work towards a shared vision. In this way, the sense of purpose helps set the direction for individual teams. Then it can move outward to provide a guiding light, helping larger parts of the organization to understand the mission, values, and goals.

Leaders who move with a clear sense of purpose, establish trust and credibility among team members and stakeholders. They see your commitment to a greater cause and are more likely to trust your leadership. This trust and credibility are essential for building strong relationships and fostering inter and intra agency collaboration.

For team members and employees, having a clear sense of purpose allows for meaningful work creation. When employees understand how their efforts contribute to the larger purpose of public service, they feel a sense of fulfillment and satisfaction in their work. This can increase their engagement, productivity, and job satisfaction.

As previously stated, a strong sense of purpose helps you and your team navigate through challenges and setbacks. It provides the resilience needed to overcome obstacles and persevere in the pursuit of your goals. During difficult times, a clear sense of purpose reminds you of the greater impact you are striving to achieve, enabling you to stay focused and motivated. If we can set our eyes on the end goal, the present difficulty becomes less like climbing mount Everest, and more like climbing a flight of stairs.

Ultimately, having a clear sense of purpose as a leader in public service enables you to make a positive impact on society. When your actions and decisions are guided by a purpose that seeks to serve the public good, you contribute to the betterment of individuals, communities, and society as a whole. This sense of purpose drives you and your team to go beyond individual goals and work towards creating positive change on a larger scale.

Wrapping up, having a clear sense of purpose as a leader in public service is vital for inspiring, motivating, and aligning your team. It guides your decision-making, builds trust and credibility, creates meaningful work, fosters resilience, promotes alignment and cohesion, and enables you to make a positive impact on society. By cultivating a clear sense of purpose, you can effectively lead your team towards achieving meaningful and impactful outcomes in public service.

Strategies for developing and communicating a compelling vision for your team

In the previous section we have discussed the necessity of having a clear purpose. The question to be asked now is, "how does a public service agency create such a vision and broadcast it successfully?". Here we will attempt to answer this question with several strategies to help leaders develop and effectively communicate a compelling vision.

Clarify Your Purpose: Start by clarifying the purpose of your team within the broader context of the organization's mission and goals. Understand the unique value your team brings to the table and how it contributes to the overall mission of public service. This clarity will form the foundation of your vision. People need to know why they are doing what they are being asked to do.

Provide Context and Rationale: Explain the context and rationale behind the vision. Help your team understand the factors driving the need for change or the opportunities that the vision presents. Providing context and rationale helps team members see the significance and urgency of the vision, fostering buy-in and commitment.

Involve Your Team: Involve your team members in the visioning process. Seek their input, ideas, and perspectives to create a shared vision that reflects their aspirations and motivates them. This collaborative approach fosters ownership and commitment from team members, making the vision more meaningful and inspiring. People need buy-in to the process. Allowing them to participate in the process creates real connections.

Define Clear Goals and Objectives: Align your vision with clear, actionable goals and objectives. Many agencies use the acronym S.M.A.R.T. to describe their goal setting process. Goals must be Specific, Measurable, Achievable, Relevant, and Time-bound. This clarity will help your team understand the direction and progress towards the vision.

Communicate with Clarity and Passion: Leaders must use compelling language to convey the purpose, values, and desired impact of the team's work. Articulate your vision with clarity and passion. Paint a vivid picture of the future state you envision, highlighting the benefits and positive outcomes. The leader's passion and enthusiasm can, and will, inspire and engage employees.

Connect the Vision to Individual Roles: Help your team members see how their individual roles and contributions directly align with the vision. Clearly communicate how each person's work connects to the larger purpose and how their efforts contribute to achieving the vision. This creates a sense of purpose and relevance, motivating team members to work towards the shared goal.

Be Open to Feedback and Adaptation: As the work proceeds, Leaders must listen to their team members' perspectives and concerns, and be willing to adapt and refine the processes, or even the vision itself based on their input. Encourage open dialogue and feedback regarding the vision. This inclusive approach strengthens the vision by incorporating diverse viewpoints and enhancing team ownership.

Reinforce and Celebrate Progress: Agencies must celebrate milestones and achievements along the way, recognizing the contributions of individual team members and the collective effort. Leaders must provide regular communication and status updates regarding progress towards the vision. This reinforces the importance of the vision, boosts morale, and maintains momentum towards its realization.

In conclusion, developing and communicating a compelling vision for your team in public service requires clarity, collaboration, effective communication, and a shared sense of purpose. By involving your team, defining clear goals, communicating with clarity and passion, connecting the vision to individual roles, providing context, being open to feedback, and reinforcing progress, you can create a compelling vision that inspires and motivates your team to achieve remarkable outcomes in public service.

Aligning your team's goals with your organization's mission and values

The next question to examine is, "How can a leader be sure that the goals for their team are supporting the overall organizational mission?". We understand that aligning your team's goals with your organization's mission and values is essential for achieving success in public service. Yet frequently we find that sections of large agencies may be unknowingly out of step with each other. To remedy this, here are several possible strategy considerations for ensuring alignment.

To begin, all involved must familiarize themselves with the mission and values of your organization. This goes double for leaders. These mission and value statements serve as guiding principles that define the purpose and desired impact of your work. Understanding them deeply is the first step towards aligning your team's goals.

Secondly, we must ensure that ensure that everyone understands the overarching purpose and the core principles that guide your organization. Leaders must communicate the organization's mission and values clearly and consistently. This clarity provides a foundation for aligning individual and team goals.

As previously stated, buy-in on the process is key. All stakeholders and team members must be engaged in the goal-setting process. Encourage them to identify how their work aligns with the organization's mission and values. By involving them, you create a sense of ownership and commitment to achieving shared objectives. This includes collaborative and cross-functional teams. Leaders need to ensure that everyone is working towards a common vision

Leaders must continuously communicate and tie-back to the vision. Reinforce the connection between your team's goals and the organization's mission and values. Regularly remind your team members how their work contributes to the larger purpose. This communication maintains focus and motivation.

In order to ensure progress toward the stated goals, Public service agencies must monitor progress and reward alignment. Advancement towards the aligned goals must be communicated to employees regularly. Monitor and report. This feedback loop enables course correction, highlights areas for improvement, and reinforces alignment with the organization's mission and values.

Further, the agency must recognize and reward alignment with the stated goals. Leaders must celebrate milestones and achievements that demonstrate improvement, and reward efforts that align with the organization's mission and values. This recognition reinforces the importance of alignment and motivates team members to continue their commitment.

Summing up, by aligning team goals with organizational mission and values, Leaders can create cohesive and purpose-driven environments in public service. This alignment ensures that individual and team efforts are focused, relevant, impactful, and contribute to the overall success of the organization. And always, in public service, the success of the organization is measured by how well we provide for the community.

Chapter 7:
Overcoming Obstacles to Excellence

"There are people whose attention is consistently drawn away from their purpose and toward their pain, like a moth to a light. Such people, who pay attention to every annoyance and obstacle in their way, are usually unsuccessful in their endeavors" -- Eric Greitans

"Obstacles are those frightful things you see when you take your eyes off your goal." – Henry Ford

Common obstacles that can prevent teams from achieving excellence

Those in public service careers often face obstacles which can hinder their ability to achieve excellence. Writer Michael Lipsky's points out in his book Street Level Bureaucrats that "Many of the challenges faced by public servants are endemic and systemic, and as a result, life for many workers is simply about getting by". For Lipsky, the often quoted "good enough for government work", is about basic survival for employees.

Understanding and addressing these challenges is crucial for overcoming them. What follows are eight common obstacles Leaders and organizations may encounter in public service.

Lack of Clear Goals and Direction: Without clearly defined goals and a shared sense of direction, individuals, teams and entire agencies may struggle to prioritize their work and make progress towards desired outcomes. It is important to establish (SMART) specific, measurable, and actionable goals that align with the organization's mission.

Inadequate Communication: Communication breakdowns can impede collaboration and hinder the flow of information within a team. When communication problems are endemic to a public service agency, important details can be missed, leading to misunderstandings, delays, and decreased productivity. Encouraging open and transparent communication is essential.

Limited Resources: Public service teams often face resource constraints, such as limited budgets, staff, or equipment. Insufficient resources can hinder their ability to deliver high-quality services and meet the needs of the community. It is important to advocate for adequate resources and seek creative solutions to maximize the impact of available resources.

Resistance to Change: Every organization is simply a collection of individual human beings. And humans are collectively resistant to change. A public service organization can be resistant to change due to bureaucratic structures, institutional inertia, or risk aversion. Regardless of the cause, this resistance can hinder innovation, adaptability, and the ability to respond to evolving needs. Encouraging a culture of continuous improvement and promoting a mindset that embraces change is crucial.

Lack of Collaboration: Otherwise called "not my problem", silos and turf wars can hinder collaboration and information sharing among teams and departments. When collaboration is lacking, duplication of efforts, inefficiencies, and missed opportunities may occur. Encouraging cross-functional collaboration, fostering a culture of teamwork, and breaking down barriers can help overcome this obstacle.

Limited Professional Development Opportunities: When team members do not have access to professional development and training opportunities, their skills and knowledge may become stagnant. This can hinder their ability to innovate and deliver high-quality services. Investing in professional development and providing learning opportunities is essential for continuous growth and improvement.

Resistance to Diversity and Inclusion: A lack of diversity and inclusion within teams can limit perspectives, creativity, and the ability to effectively serve a diverse community. Overcoming biases, promoting diversity, and creating an inclusive environment where all team members feel valued and heard is vital for achieving excellence in public service.

Ineffective Leadership: Leadership plays a critical role in guiding and supporting teams. Ineffective leadership can lead to low morale, lack of direction, and a loss of motivation among team members. Strong leadership that fosters a positive work culture, provides guidance, and empowers team members is crucial for overcoming obstacles and achieving excellence.

Strategies for overcoming these obstacles

Now that we have identified many of the common obstacles, we should examine strategies for remedying them. Achieving excellence in public service requires implementing effective strategies in communication, problem-solving, and conflict resolution. Here are a few strategies to address these challenges.

Right People, Right Places: All the strategies outlined below can be negated by an organization having personnel in misplaced roles. Simply put, an organization must invest the time in placing employees where they can be most effective. Additionally, leaders and managers in public service must be promoted and re-assigned based upon behavioral alignment with the organizational goals. This agency behavior establishes a clear statement that moving the goals and vision forward results in upward mobility.

Enhance Communication: Establish clear channels of communication within the team, and throughout the organization. Leaders must ensure that information flows freely and transparently. Encourage active listening and open dialogue to promote understanding and collaboration. Regularly update team members on progress, changes, and expectations to avoid misunderstandings and confusion.

Foster a Culture of Problem-Solving: Leaders must encourage a problem-solving mindset within the agency. Create a safe space for brainstorming ideas, sharing perspectives, and exploring innovative solutions. Foster an organizational culture that values critical thinking, creativity, and continuous improvement. Empower team members to take ownership of challenges and facilitate collaborative problem-solving sessions.

Develop Conflict Resolution Skills: Conflict is inevitable, but how it is managed determines its impact on team dynamics. Public agencies must invest in conflict resolution training to equip team members with effective communication and negotiation skills. Encourage open dialogue, active listening, and finding win-win solutions. Mediation or facilitation techniques can also help resolve conflicts in a neutral and constructive manner.

Promote Collaboration: Breaking down silos and encouraging cross-functional collaboration must be an organizational priority. Leaders must facilitate an environment where team members feel comfortable reaching out to others for support, sharing knowledge, and working together towards common goals.

Emphasize the value of collective intelligence and celebrate successful collaborations to reinforce its importance.

Establish Clear Roles and Responsibilities: Ambiguity regarding roles and responsibilities can lead to confusion and decreased productivity. The agency must clearly define each team member's roles, expectations, and areas of accountability. Regularly review and realign roles as necessary to ensure efficiency and minimize overlaps or gaps.

Lead by Example: Leaders play a crucial role in overcoming obstacles. They must demonstrate effective communication, problem-solving, and conflict resolution skills in their own actions and interactions. Leaders must act as a role model for the team, exhibiting a collaborative and solution-oriented approach. Encourage open dialogue, invite feedback, and address conflicts constructively.

Regularly Evaluate and Adjust: Public service organizations must continuously assess team dynamics and performance to identify areas for improvement. Leaders need to seek feedback from team members on communication, problem-solving, and conflict resolution processes. Adapt strategies and approaches based on the team's needs and changing circumstances. Regularly review and update team protocols to enhance effectiveness.

By implementing these strategies, teams in public service can overcome common obstacles, foster effective communication, enhance problem-solving skills, and resolve conflicts constructively. This enables them to work cohesively towards achieving excellence in their service delivery and making a positive impact on the communities they serve.

Dealing with failure and setbacks in a productive way

Having a framework to for dealing with failure and setbacks in a productive way is essential for teams in public service to maintain resilience and continue making meaningful progress. Former professional basketball player Kobe Bryant once said that for him, "…failure is exciting. It gives me a measurement of where I am, and all the things I need to work on". In short, Kobe's mindset and process was attuned to see potentially frustrating setbacks as growth opportunities.

What follows is a discussion of various strategies for effectively handling failure and setbacks in a productive manner. Leaders would be wise to seek ways to turn setbacks, into setups for future progress.

The first step in this process is for the agency to encourage a growth mindset. Leaders must remember to encourage team members to view failure and setbacks as opportunities for learning and growth. Emphasize that mistakes are a natural part of the process and provide a safe environment where team members feel comfortable discussing and reflecting on their failures.

The second organizational step is to urge reflection and analysis once failures happen. After experiencing a setback, encourage the team to reflect on what went wrong and why. Facilitate open discussions to analyze the root causes and identify lessons learned. Encourage team members to share their insights and take collective responsibility for identifying improvements.

Thirdly, to deal setbacks in a productive way, the agency must emphasize continuous improvement. Use setbacks as a catalyst for ongoing development. Encourage the team to brainstorm ideas and innovative solutions to overcome the challenges they faced. Leaders must push the culture to embrace change and encourage experimentation to find new approaches.

Fourth, during times of failure or setbacks, it is important to offer support and encouragement to team members. Recognize their efforts and the lessons they have learned. Provide resources, training, or mentorship to help them develop the skills needed to overcome future challenges.

At this point, we need to emphasize that none of the above strategies can succeed without maintaining open communication throughout the organization. Our fifth strategy here is that leaders need to maintain an environment where team members feel safe to share their failures and setbacks openly. Encourage honest and transparent communication to facilitate learning from mistakes and foster a sense of trust and psychological safety within the team.

Strategy number six is for the agency to set realistic expectations. Leaders must ensure that team members have a clear understanding of what success looks like; and what realistic goals and timelines are. Unrealistic expectations can and will set the team up for failure. By setting achievable goals, team members can better manage setbacks and maintain motivation.

Next, leaders must focus on solutions, not blame when failures happen. Instead of finger pointing, shift the focus to finding solutions. Create a blame-free environment that promotes collaboration and problem-solving. Encourage the team to work together to identify the root causes and develop action plans to overcome challenges.

Lastly, it is important to celebrate both small and significant successes along the way. Recognize the efforts and achievements of the team, even in the face of challenges. Celebrating milestones and progress reinforces a positive mindset and motivates team members to persevere.

By implementing these strategies, teams in public service can effectively navigate failures and setbacks, turning them into opportunities for growth, innovation, and continuous improvement. This approach fosters resilience, strengthens team cohesion, and ultimately enhances the team's ability to deliver impactful services to the public

Chapter 8:
Sustaining Excellence

"Leadership is about making others better as a result of your presence and making sure that impact lasts in your absence." - Sheryl Sandberg

How to sustain a culture of excellence over time

At this point in our ongoing discussion of making room for excellence, we need to examine how to continue to sustain a culture of excellence once the organization succeeds in building it. All our progress can be undone if agencies do not make sustaining choices in how business is conducted.

In short, maintaining excellence in public service over time requires ongoing commitment and strategic efforts. Here are some of the key strategies to help maintain and foster a culture of excellence in the long term.

Leaders play a pivotal role in sustaining a culture of excellence. They must lead by example, consistently demonstrating and upholding the values and behaviors that define excellence. They must set high standards for their own performance and hold themselves accountable. Leaders must be willing to act as a role model for the team, exhibiting a strong work ethic, integrity, and a commitment to continuous improvement.

As an ongoing matter, leaders within the agency must clearly define and communicate the standards of excellence expected. Establish goals, performance metrics, and quality benchmarks that align with the organization's mission and values. Provide regular feedback and recognition to reinforce the importance of maintaining high standards.

As an additional ongoing concern, leaders within the agency must encourage a culture of continuous learning and professional development. Encourage team members to seek out new ideas, stay informed about industry trends, and apply innovative approaches to their work. The organization must offer opportunities for training, workshops, and knowledge sharing to enhance skills and keep up with evolving best practices.

Next, if a public service agency wants to maintain excellence, they must continue to promote collaboration and teamwork. Leaders must encourage open communication, information sharing, and cross-functional collaboration. Foster an environment where team members work together towards common goals. Create opportunities for team members to collaborate on projects, exchange ideas, and leverage each other's strengths to achieve better outcomes.

Collaboration increases opportunities for innovation and creativity. Leaders must embrace this for the long haul by creating channels for idea generation and provide resources for experimenting with new approaches. This enables the entire agency to support and empower employees to take appropriate risks and explore innovative solutions for improved service delivery.

Further, the agency must continually acknowledge and celebrate exemplary performance and achievements within the team. Leaders should implement and support a system of recognition and rewards that incentivizes and motivates team members to strive for excellence. Publicly highlight and appreciate the contributions of individuals and teams who consistently demonstrate outstanding performance.

The organization must also establish and maintain mechanisms for gathering feedback from team members, stakeholders, and the public. Actively seeking feedback and input supports sustained excellence by identifying areas for improvement. Leaders must regularly evaluate team processes, systems, and performance to drive continuous improvement and ensure that excellence remains a priority.

The final sustaining strategy is for the agency to create long lasting excellence is to maintain a positive and supportive work environment. This environment must promotes well-being, engagement, and a sense of belonging. Leaders must encourage and demonstrate work-life balance, provide employees with growth opportunities, and demonstrate respect, and inclusivity. When employees feel valued and supported, they are more likely to be motivated and committed to delivering excellence.

By implementing the aforementioned behavioral changes, public service organizations can sustain a culture of excellence over time. This fosters a high-performing and engaged team, delivers exceptional services to the public, and contributes to the overall success and reputation of the organization.

The importance of remaining flexible as a leader

Adapting to changing circumstances and remaining flexible is crucial for leaders in public service to effectively navigate complex challenges and achieve success. Organizational capacity to deal with the unexpected must established and maintained.

The public service landscape is constantly evolving due to various factors such as technological advancements, social changes, and economic shifts. Leaders must adapt to these dynamic environments to ensure their organizations remain relevant and responsive to the needs of the public. As the expectations of citizens and stakeholders are continuously evolving, agencies must remain able to meet new needs. Leaders need to understand and anticipate these changing expectations to deliver services that align with the evolving demands of the community. Adapting to changing circumstances allows leaders to meet these expectations effectively.

This can only happen by embracing Innovation. Remaining adaptable and flexible enables leaders to embrace innovation and leverage new technologies, strategies, and approaches. By being open to change, leaders can foster a culture of innovation within their organizations, encouraging creativity and continuous improvement.

The uncertain is a veritable certainty. Public service often involves dealing with complex and unpredictable situations. Leaders who can adapt to changing circumstances are better equipped to manage uncertainty, make informed decisions, and navigate through complexities effectively.

The two best ways to deal with uncertainty are by building organizational resilience and maximizing opportunities. Regarding resilience, the agency must be able to adjust strategies when necessary while maintaining an overall sense of optimism. Being able to adapt to changing circumstances allows leaders to maintain forward momentum even in the face of adversity.

Concerning maximizing opportunities, leaders must be ready and able to seize new opportunities to advance the agency that may arise. By being open to change and willing to explore different possibilities, leaders can capitalize on emerging trends, partnerships, and innovative approaches that can lead to positive outcomes for their organizations and the communities they serve.

When employees see their leaders being flexible and adaptable, they are more likely to be engaged and motivated. By embracing change and fostering a culture of flexibility, leaders inspire their teams to embrace new ideas, learn new skills, and contribute to the overall success of the organization. This of course has multiple positive outcomes, as the individual, group and community are all better served.

But perhaps the best possible result from leadership flexibility is for the organization and leader themselves to maintain relevance and longevity: In a rapidly changing world, organizations that fail to adapt become stagnant and risk becoming irrelevant. And managers who fail to adapt, often are pushed out for more vibrant possibilities. Leaders who prioritize adaptability and flexibility ensure the long-term sustainability and success of their organizations by staying ahead of the curve and responding effectively to emerging trends and challenges.

In summary, as a leader in public service, it is crucial to adapt to changing circumstances and remain flexible. Embracing adaptability allows leaders to respond to dynamic environments, meet changing expectations, embrace innovation, manage uncertainty, build resilience, maximize opportunities, enhance employee engagement, and maintain relevance over the long term. By embracing these qualities, leaders can lead their organizations to navigate through challenges successfully and achieve their missions of serving the public effectively.

Chapter 9: Conclusion

"Fight for the things that you care about, but do it in a way that will lead others to join you." - Ruth Bader Ginsburg

Summary of key points

In writing this book, my intention was to present a thought-provoking set of arguments that delve into the key principles and strategies needed to foster excellence within public service organizations. The target audience for this documentation being leaders, leadership students, managers, and other individuals working in the public sector.

If there is nothing else that you remember when you are done with this book, I want you to remember the following key points:

1. Being a manager isn't enough. Be an actual leader. People in these positions must be expected to do the work of demonstrating visionary thinking, empathy, and the ability to empower and motivate others. Be flexible and responsive.
2. Leaders must set a clear vision and mission for public service organizations. Communicate the vision and align team goals with it.
3. Leaders must create a culture of continuous improvement and innovation; where individuals

are encouraged to challenge the status quo and embrace change.
4. Leaders must develop institutional capacity for attracting, developing, and retaining top talent in public service.
5. Diversity, Equity and Inclusion (DEI) = opportunities for all employees to be more likely to achieve excellence.
6. Teamwork and Collaboration sets the table for diverse perspectives, problem-solving and better decision-making.
7. Communication, Communication, Communication. You cannot over-communicate what is happening, what is needed, and progress towards the big goals.
8. Technology is your friend. Use it to streamline your processes.

Final Thoughts

How do you see yourself?

Fundamentally, if we ever want to see real progress in creating a culture of excellence within public service organizations, we need to change the way that people see themselves. As employees of such entities, we need to move ourselves away from simply being our various job titles and move into leadership. It's not enough to just be a team lead, supervisor, manager, or etc. We need to start seeing ourselves as leaders with a responsibility to others, including the public. Good enough for government work, just isn't good enough for government work anymore.

We need to challenge ourselves to be bold enough to seek what is actually possible. What would be accomplished if you truly applied yourself and did more than the minimal?

How do you see them?

When you look at your team how do you see them? Are they valuable individuals who need to be coached and helped to achieve the best version of themselves? Are they real and complete human beings? Or do you see them as something else?

One of the worst traits of managers in my estimation is to see people as things. Like tools or widgets to simply be used to get the work done. What I'm calling for is a radical overhaul in this thinking process. We need to love people and use things instead of the other way around. Our co-workers need compassion. Balance this with accountability for great results.

How do you see the work?

When we look at the work of public servants we must remember that the end goal is always a better, safer community for all. This can be difficult when you find yourself locked in the mundane routine that makes up your everyday job. How does filing documents properly or sending emails equate to safer neighborhoods?

If we can find ways to connect the individual efforts of what we do to the big picture goals of true service, then we can reframe our efforts. Sweeping the floor now becomes more than just sweeping the floor. It's a way of ensuring that people are safe and cared about. Leaders must continually reframe the work as meaningful and important to the everyday citizenry.

<u>Critical need for internal communication</u>

We have a desperate and critical need for communication throughout the field of public service. Far too frequently we find civil servants that have little idea of what it is they're actually supposed to be doing... And whom it benefits. This disconnection can only occur in an environment in which the mission is not communicated.

Public service organizations need to ensure that communication flows in all directions. Staff need to be able to express concerns to management and have them heard and taken seriously. Managers must not be information hoarders, rather, sharing the flow of what is going on readily and without reservation.

Desperate for transparency & trust

Externally, public service organizations must seek to achieve greater transparency. The same communication breakdowns that happen internally, leading to confusion, inequity, and waste will utterly destroy public trust externally.

The community are the taxpayers whose dollars the public servant uses for salary, equipment, training, etc. These people can and will expect an accounting of what was done with public funds. Any amount of mismanagement or hesitation to answer the call for transparency will lead to public outrage in our current cancel-culture obsessed climate.

The audacity of hope

Yes, I "borrowed" the title of Barack Obama's book. However, I think that it is appropriate given what I'm about to say.

First, the current political climate which is calling for accountability and shaming any organization that fails to meet public demands can actually be part of a positive change process. We can wilt under the examination of the public eye and media scrutiny, or we can use this as an opportunity to be better.

If an agency can demonstrate that they are doing as they are supposed, in the best possible way, they instantly rise to the top levels of respect and recognition in their profession. This type of performance becomes the content of subject-matter-expert, conference presentations, academic journal articles, and social media posts.

Secondly, public opinion is changing with regards to the employer to employee relationship. Some of this is due to millennials and Gen Z individuals entering the workforce and demanding more of a work life balance. Another portion of it is the social upheavals that happened in the wake of COVID-19, Black lives matter, and a far more visible LGBTQ inclusivity movement.

These people want to be seen. They want to be heard. And most of all, they want to be treated as people, not objects. These employees will not wait around for decision makers to eventually decide to offer growth opportunities. They will simply hand in their two weeks notice.

Why do I see this as a good thing? Because the pressure of keeping public agencies staffed and equipped will undoubtedly cause leaders to change policy and practice. Whether they want to or not, they will have to consider modifying the way business as usual has been conducted. Public service organizations will have to consider telework, other flexible work schedules, mentoring and development opportunities, enhanced training programs and college tuition paybacks.

I believe changes like those referenced in this book are a beginning for a paradigm shift in our understanding of American public service. My sincere hope is that I have contributed in some small way.

www.ingramcontent.com/pod-product-compliance
Lightning Source LLC
Chambersburg PA
CBHW031431210526
45464CB00005B/2151